ALFRED'S BASIC ADULT PIANO COURSE

GREATEST HITS

Movies

Selected and Edited by E. L. Lancaster & Morton Manus

This new series answers the often expressed need for a variety of supplementary material in many different popular styles. What could be more fun for an adult than to play the music that everybody knows and loves? The remarkable part of this new *Greatest Hits* series is that soon after beginning piano study, anyone can play attractive versions of the best-known music of today.

This book is correlated page-by-page with Lesson Book 3 of Alfred's Basic Adult Piano Course; pieces should be assigned based on the instructions in the upper-right corner of each title page of *Greatest Hits* (the correlation for Alfred's Adult All-in-One Course is included in parentheses).

Since the melodies and rhythms of popular music do not always lend themselves to precise grading, you may find that these pieces are sometimes a little more difficult than the corresponding pages in the Lesson Book. The teacher's judgment is the most important factor in deciding when to begin each title.

When the books in the *Greatest Hits* series are assigned in conjunction with the Lesson Books, these appealing pieces reinforce new concepts as they are introduced. In addition, the motivation the music provides could not be better. The emotional satisfaction students receive from mastering each popular song increases their enthusiasm to begin the next one. With the popular music available in the *Greatest Hits* series (Levels 1, 2 and 3), the use of all three books will significantly increase every adult's interest in piano study.

Published by

Distributed by
Alfred Publishing Co., Inc.

ISBN 0-7390-1644-X

Cover photos: Piano © Karen Miller • Movie film reel © PhotoDisc, Inc. • Background lights © Eyewire
Backgrounds © PhotoDisc, Inc. (right and lower right panels, back cover); © Eyewire (bottom center)
Marquee light © Ted Engelbart • Times Square © Corbis

Getting to Know You

from THE KING AND I

Use with Alfred's Basic Adult Piano Course,
LESSON BOOK, LEVEL 2, after page 4
(or with Alfred's Adult All-in-One Course, after page 4).

Lyrics by Oscar Hammerstein II
Music by Richard Rodgers
Arr. by Martha Mier

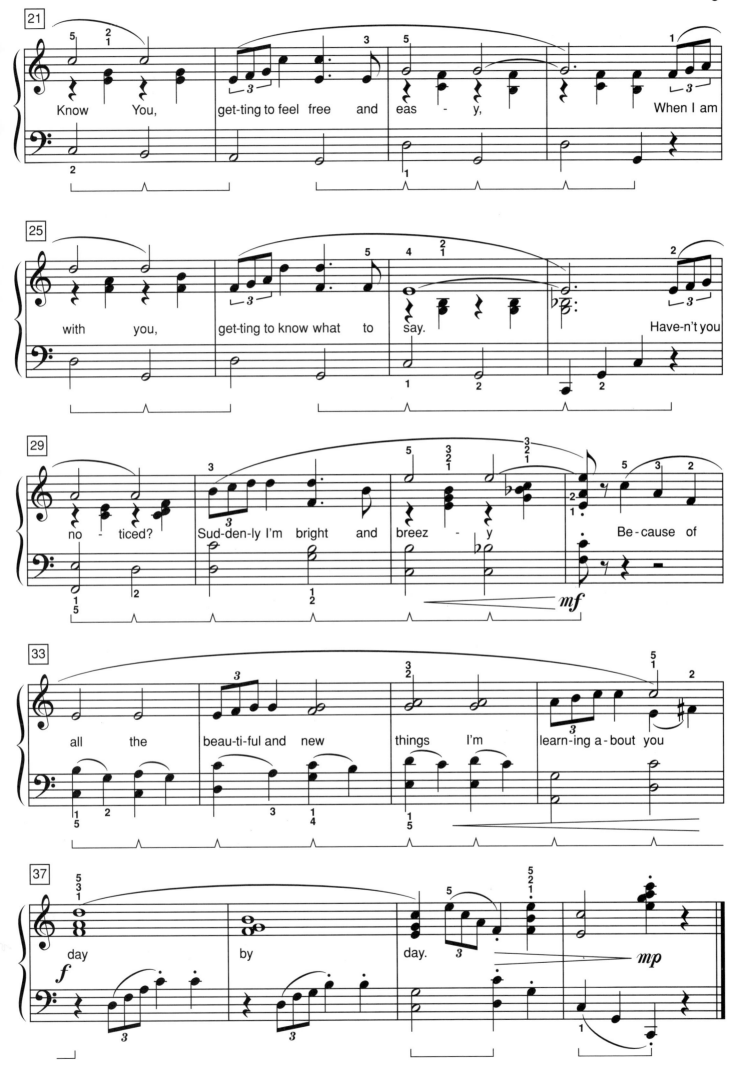

The Odd Couple

Theme from the Paramount Television Series THE ODD COUPLE

Words by Sammy Cahn
Music by Neal Hefti
Arr. by Tom Gerou

Can't Help Falling in Love

from the Paramount Picture BLUE HAWAII

Words and Music by
George David Weiss, Hugo Peretti and Luigi Creatore
Arr. by Catherine Rollin

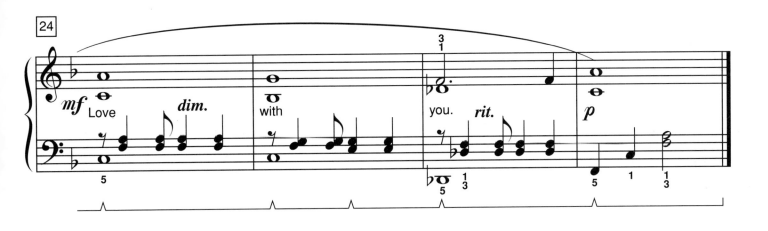

I Love Lucy

from the Television Series

Lyric by Harold Adamson
Music by Eliot Daniel
Arr. by Tom Gerou

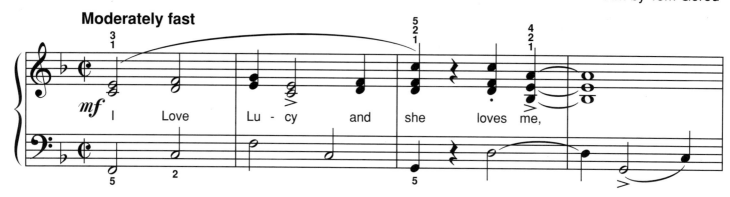

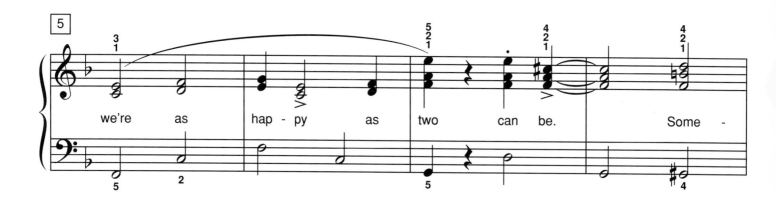

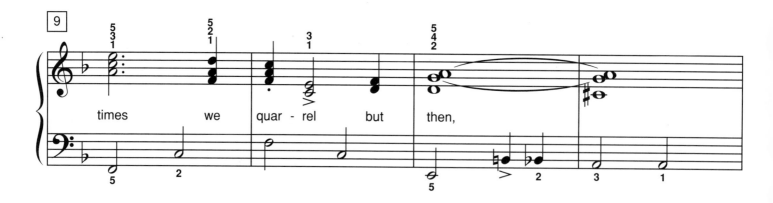

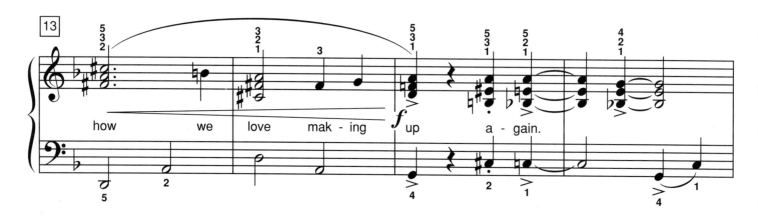

Speak Softly, Love (Love Theme)

from the Paramount Picture THE GODFATHER

Words by Larry Kusik
Music by Nino Rota
Arr. by Martha Mier

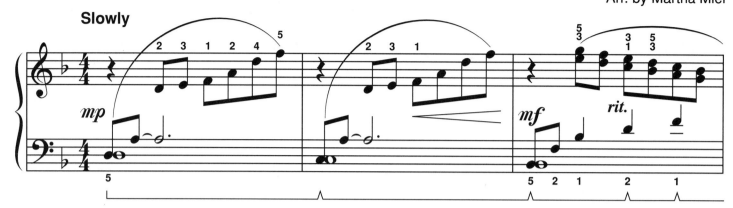

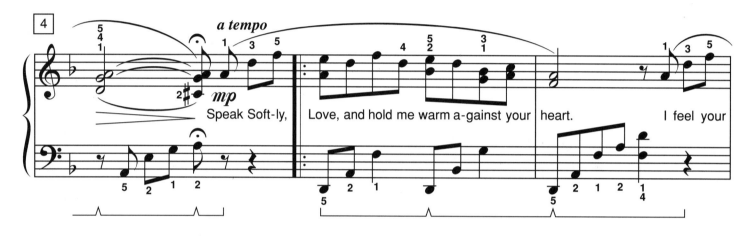

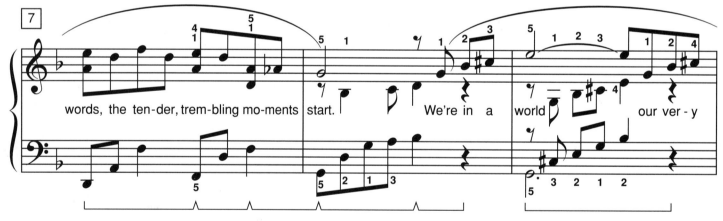

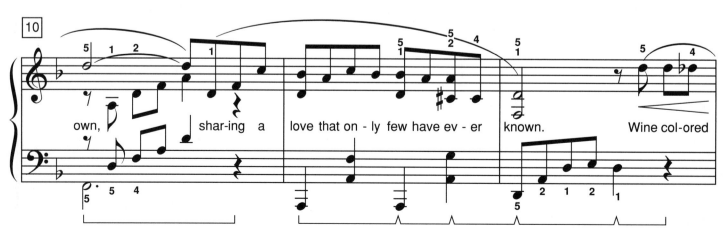

Y.M.C.A.

Words and Music by
Jacques Morali, Henri Belolo and Victor Willis
Arr. by George Peter Tingley

Use after page 30 (50).

Till There Was You

from Meredith Willson's THE MUSIC MAN

By Meredith Willson
Arr. by Catherine Rollin

A Time for Us (Love Theme)

from the Paramount Picture ROMEO AND JULIET

Words by Larry Kusik and Eddie Snyder
Music by Nino Rota
Arr. by Sharon Aaronson

Slowly and expressively

You'll Be in My Heart (Pop Version)

from Walt Disney Pictures' TARZAN™

Words and Music by Phil Collins
Arr. by Tom Gerou

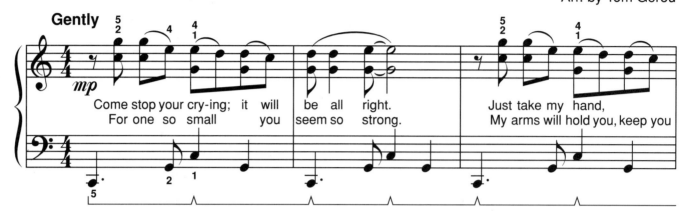

Come stop your cry-ing; it will be all right. Just take my hand,
For one so small you seem so strong. My arms will hold you, keep you

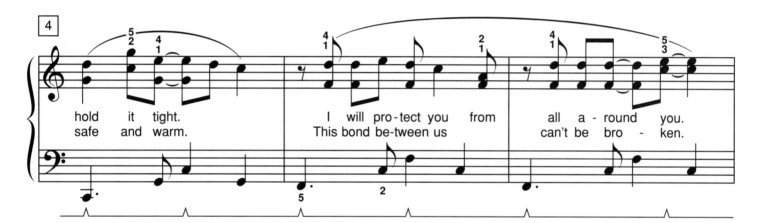

hold it tight. I will pro-tect you from all a-round you.
safe and warm. This bond be-tween us can't be bro - ken.

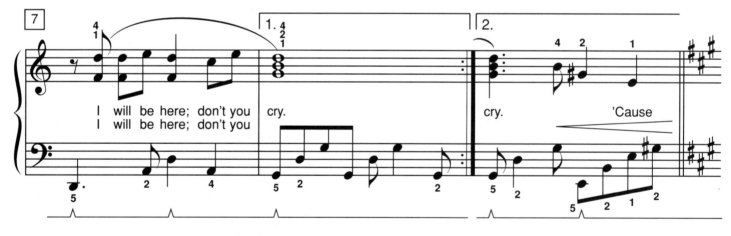

I will be here; don't you cry.
I will be here; don't you cry. 'Cause

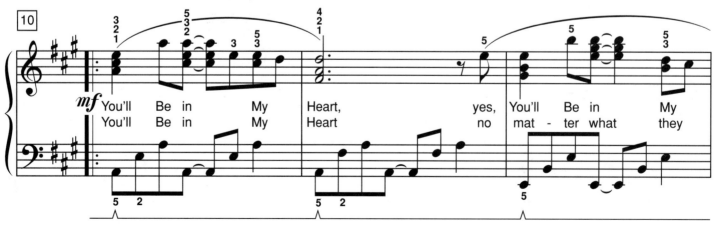

You'll Be in My Heart, yes, You'll Be in My
You'll Be in My Heart no mat - ter what they

The Way We Were

from the Motion Picture THE WAY WE WERE

Words by Alan and Marilyn Bergman
Music by Marvin Hamlisch
Arr. by Margaret Goldston

Slowly, with great expression

22

Where Do I Begin (Love Theme)

from the Paramount Picture LOVE STORY

Words by Carl Sigman
Music by Francis Lai
Arr. by Sharon Aaronson

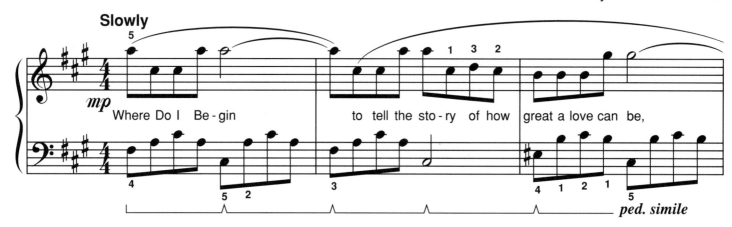

Where Do I Be-gin to tell the sto-ry of how great a love can be,

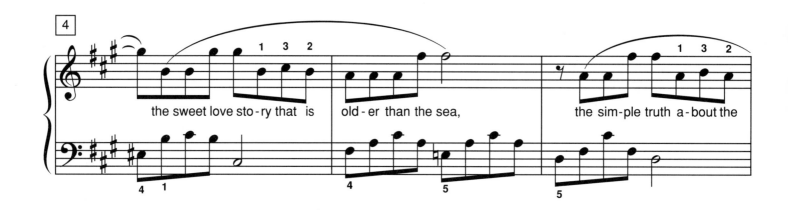

the sweet love sto-ry that is old-er than the sea, the sim-ple truth a-bout the

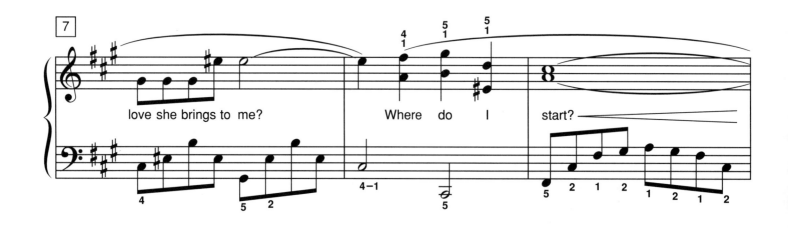

love she brings to me? Where do I start?

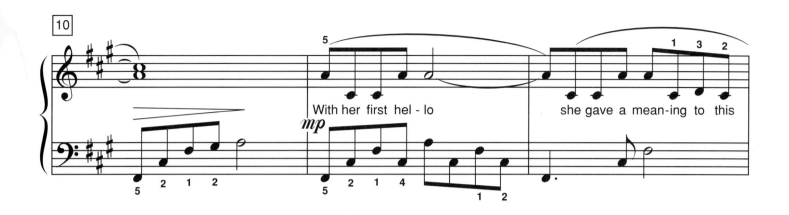

How long does it last? Can love be meas-ured by the hours in a day?

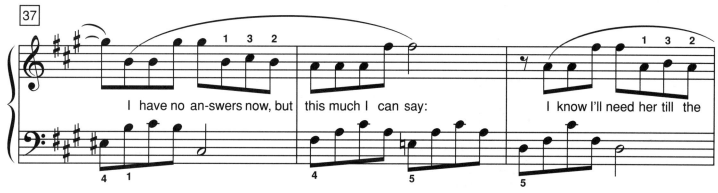

I have no an-swers now, but this much I can say: I know I'll need her till the

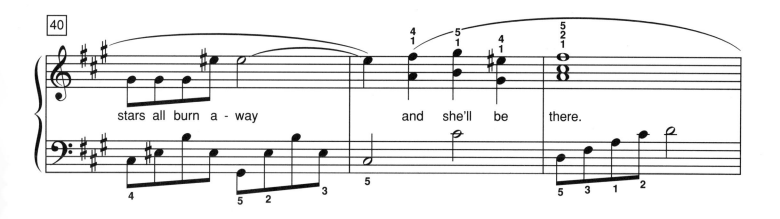

stars all burn a-way and she'll be there.

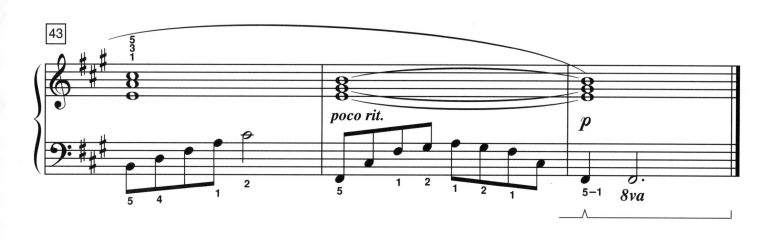

When I Fall in Love

from ONE MINUTE TO ZERO

Words by Edward Heyman
Music by Victor Young
Arr. by Dennis Alexander

Puttin' on the Ritz

from the Motion Picture PUTTIN' ON THE RITZ

Words and Music by Irving Berlin
Arr. by Martha Mier

She Loves You

Words and Music by
John Lennon and Paul McCartney
Arr. by Christine H. Barden

Moderately, with a strong beat

Use after page 52 (94).

34

Wishing You Were Somehow Here Again

from THE PHANTOM OF THE OPERA

Music by Andrew Lloyd Webber
Lyrics by Charles Hart
Additional Lyrics by Richard Stilgoe
Arr. by Dennis Alexander

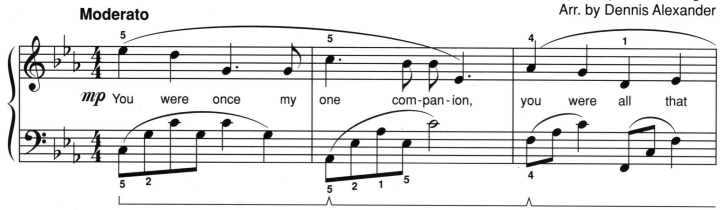

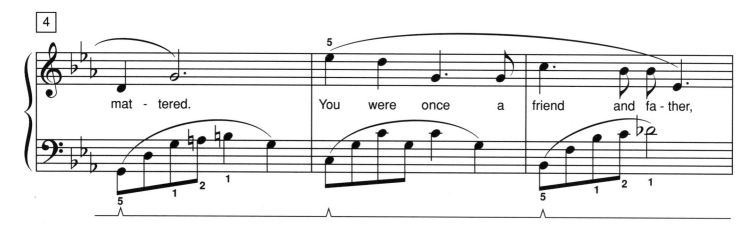

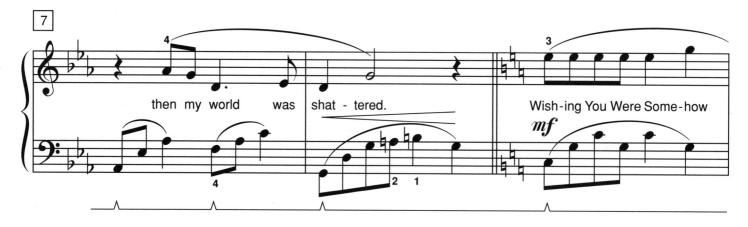

some - times it seemed   if   I   just dreamed,   some - how you would   be

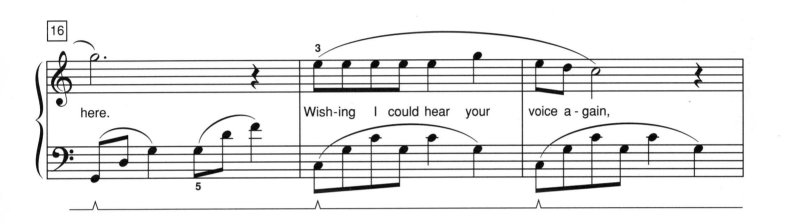

here.   Wish-ing   I could hear   your   voice a - gain,

know-ing that I nev - er   would,   dream - ing of you   won't

help   me to do   all that you dreamed   I   could.

My Funny Valentine

from BABES IN ARMS

Words by Lorenz Hart
Music by Richard Rodgers
Arr. by Sharon Aaronson

Use after page 60 (112).

Splish Splash

Words and Music by Bobby Darin and Murray Kaufman
Arr. by George Peter Tingley

Moderate rock tempo

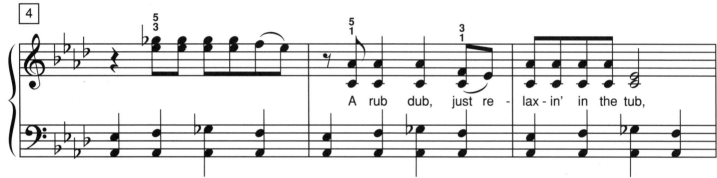

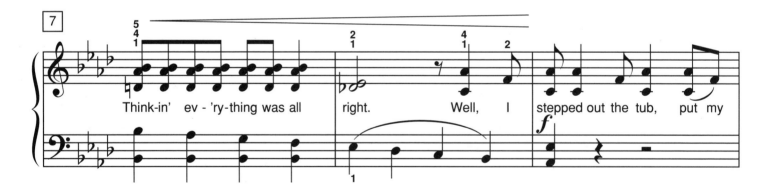

Splish Splash, I jumped back in the bath, Well, how was I to know there was a

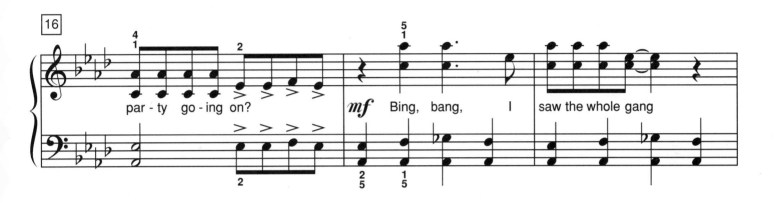

par - ty go - ing on? Bing, bang, I saw the whole gang

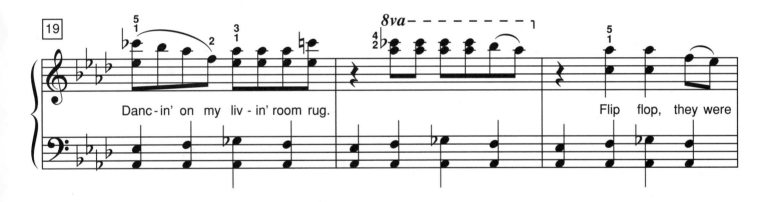

Danc - in' on my liv - in' room rug. Flip flop, they were

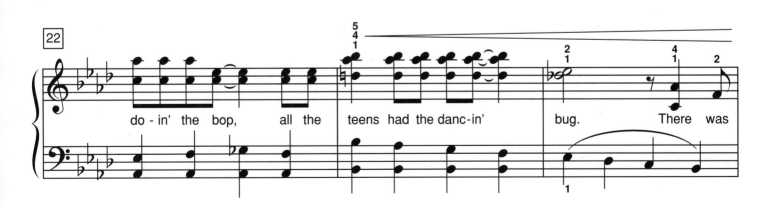

do - in' the bop, all the teens had the danc - in' bug. There was

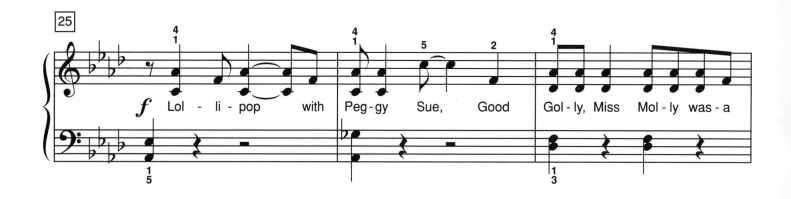

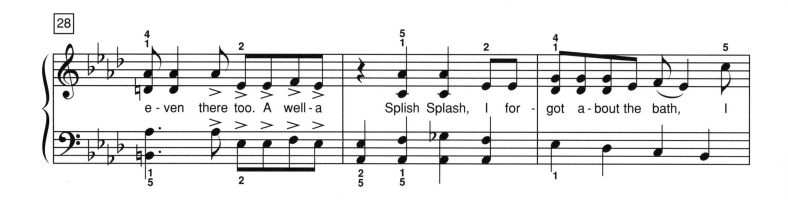

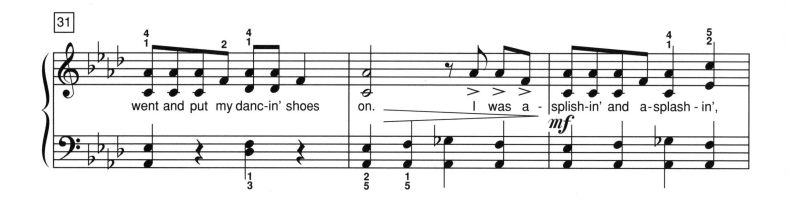

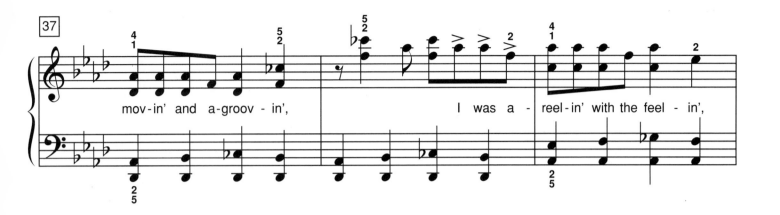

mov-in' and a-groov - in', I was a - reel-in' with the feel - in',

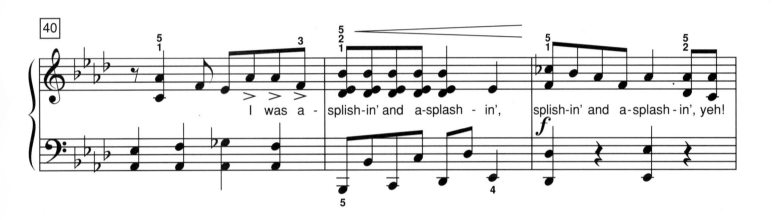

I was a - splish-in' and a-splash - in', splish-in' and a-splash - in', yeh!

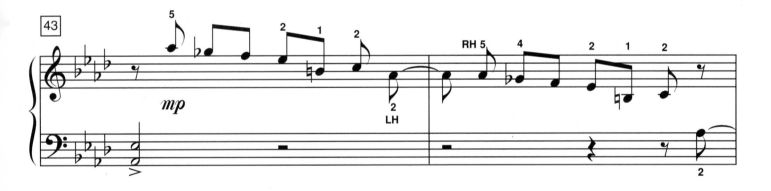

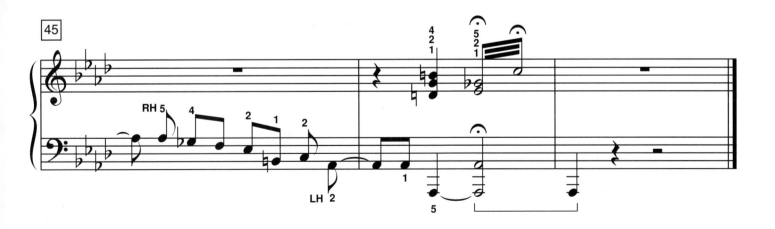

Blue Bayou

Words and Music by
Roy Orbison and Joe Melson
Arr. by Tom Gerou

Moderately slow

Use after page 74 (122).

I Dreamed a Dream

from LES MISÉRABLES

Music by Claude-Michel Schönberg
Lyrics by Herbert Kretzmer
Original Text by Alain Boublil and Jean-Marc Natel
Arr. by Dennis Alexander

Written in the Stars

from Walt Disney Theatrical Productions' AIDA

Music by Elton John
Lyrics by Tim Rice
Arr. by Sharon Aaronson

Use after page 74 (122).

Reflection

from Walt Disney Pictures' MULAN

Music by Matthew Wilder
Lyrics by David Zippel
Arr. by Martha Mier